OKEHAMPTON CASTLE

Devon

Alan Endacott

Okehampton Castle was strategically situated by its Norman builders in the heart of Devon on a spur of high ground above the valley of the River Okement. It first provided the Norman conquerors with a dramatic symbol of their new power and a defended administrative centre. Throughout the Middle Ages it provided luxurious accommodation for the Courtenay family who entertained guests here while enjoying hunting parties in the adjacent deer park.

The ruins of the Norman keep, high on its motte, can still be explored and stunning views enjoyed across Okehampton, the former deer park and north Dartmoor. Extensive parts of the medieval guest lodgings, great hall, kitchens and chapel still remain and tell a fascinating story of medieval castle development and rebuilding, as well as of castle life.

This new guidebook provides a colourful tour and history of the site, describing its architectural detail; its geology and topography and the intriguing tales of the great families who lived here.

Shield of Henry Courtenay, 9th earl of Devon and Marquis of Exeter, owner of Okehampton Castle

❖ CONTENTS ❖

Acknowledgements

The author would like to thank the following: Powderham Castle for allowing photography of the Courtenay family shields, the portrait of Henry Courtenay, 9th Earl of Devon and the castle itself; the Museum of Dartmoor Life in Okehampton for information on the bells and allowing them to be photographed; and the editor, Louise Wilson, for her help and support. He also acknowledges the extensive research conducted over the past 30 years by various people, including Dr. R.A. Higham, formerly Senior Lecturer in Archaeology at the University of Exeter, Mr. J.P. Allan, Curator of Antiquities at the Royal Albert Memorial Museum, Exeter and Mr. S.R. Blaylock of Exeter Archaeology, without whom our knowledge of the development of Okehampton Castle would be far less rich.

Published by English Heritage,
1 Waterhouse Square, 138-142 Holborn, London EC1N 2ST
Visit our website at www.english-heritage.org.uk
Commissioned and edited by Louise Wilson
Design: Clifford Manlow
Picture research: Diana Phillips
Printed in England by Park Communications Ltd
© English Heritage 2003. First published by English
Heritage 2003, revised reprint 2009, reprinted 2011

C20, 9/11, 04961, ISBN 978-1-85074-825-0
Photographs by English Heritage Photographic Unit and
copyright of English Heritage, unless otherwise stated.

TOUR OF THE CASTLE

THE BARBICAN

Leave the kiosk and ascend the two short flights of steps.

You are standing in the remains of the castle's barbican or outer gatehouse. Constructed as part of the castle's major rebuilding in about 1300, this would have functioned as the first line of defence if ever the castle came under attack. A chamber above the gate contained a garderobe or latrine, suggesting that it was occupied, possibly as a guardroom. The purpose of the pit in the corner is unknown. The barbican walls are constructed mostly of local rock with a rubble in-fill. Like most of the castle's structures, these would have been covered with lime plaster inside and out, apart from the dressed blocks which formed the surrounds of doors and windows, giving a striking appearance to anyone approaching. Here the door jambs are made from a densely grained igneous rock called aplite, which is found at Meldon, 2.4km (1.5 miles) to the south-west. An indication of the decorative detail of these is still visible on the surviving column. Small rectangular holes can be seen running

The steps leading up to the barbican or outer gatehouse

The inner gatehouse and ruins of the keep in the distance, from the barbican passage

Reconstruction drawing of the castle bailey and gatehouse from the keep, as it may have looked in the 14th century, by Terry Ball

through the walls throughout the castle. Known as putlogs (from the verb 'to put log') these were used by the builders to support their scaffolding poles during construction, before being plastered over.

The cobbling inside the barbican probably dates from the late seventeenth century when parts of the castle ruins were briefly re-occupied and altered in connection with the operation of a bakehouse in one of the old lodgings.

Continue up the slope through the barbican passage.

The same view of the ruined castle as it is today

Here, constricted between two high walls, any attackers succeeding in getting through the barbican gate would be highly vulnerable to arrows fired from the main gatehouse.

Notice the stone roof tiles of the projecting garderobe to the left of the gatehouse.

The flanking walls as you approach the gatehouse probably enclosed a pit over which a drawbridge could be lowered. The mechanism for this would have been housed in the chamber above, which may also have provided accommodation for a constable or gatekeeper. *Enter the gatehouse.* The six recesses in the walls once contained columns made of Beerstone, a soft limestone from south-east Devon, forming a vaulted ceiling.

Turn right, and walk through the gap into the adjacent chamber.

This room is an irregular shape, due to the slope on its northern side. The defensive curtain wall which formed its third side has now largely collapsed over the bank. However, you can still see the remains of a large splayed window similar to those found elsewhere on the ground floor of the castle. To your left you can see the tall gable end of the great hall, and joist holes which supported another floor above. Access to the upper floor and the chamber over the gatehouse was via the stairs in the corner. Projecting stones or corbels higher up on the gable wall supported a shallow-pitched lead roof. This room may have been an office for the castle steward or may have provided further accommodation, while the ground floor may have functioned as a guardroom and antechamber to the great hall. It is likely that commoners with business at the castle, such as tenants attending court, would have had to wait here.

Ascend the steps in the corner and enter the great hall.

THE GREAT HALL

This large hall, open to the roof, was the social and business centre of the castle and was therefore designed to impress. A massive timber-framed slate roof was supported on large timber crucks (huge curved timbers); the sockets for some of the timber roof supports can be seen in the gable

The chamber next to the gatehouse, showing the exterior of the north-eastern wall of the great hall

The steps in the corner of the chamber, leading to the great hall

The inside of the north-eastern wall of the great hall with the remains of the raised platform and hearth on the floor in front of it

This reconstruction of the great hall at Dover Castle in the 14th century must be similar to a feasting scene in the great hall at Okehampton at this time (Terry Ball)

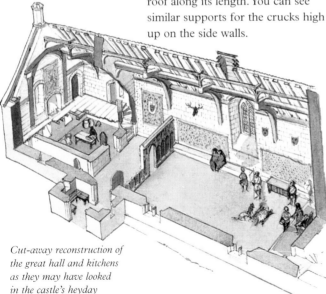

Cut-away reconstruction of the great hall and kitchens as they may have looked in the castle's heyday

ends of the hall. The timber crucks may have rested on stone corbels in the large recesses at the base of the sockets and would have braced the roof along its length. You can see similar supports for the crucks high up on the side walls.

On the floor, the remains of a low wall are visible, running parallel to the north gable wall where you entered the hall. This once formed a low platform or dais where the high table would have stood and where the lord would have sat when courts were in session. The depression in the floor in front of this is the remains of an open hearth, probably formed to melt lead after the castle was abandoned in the sixteenth century. Another open hearth nearby would have provided warmth and some of the light when the hall was in use, with the smoke filtering through a flap in the roof above.

A stone bench once ran along the outside wall, and a window high above it allowed light in over the curtain wall beyond. The windows on the opposite side are somewhat lower and would have been filled with decorative glass. The main entrance from the bailey (courtyard) is also in this wall. The degree of decoration on the door jambs here and elsewhere in the hall gives another indication of its high status. Slots for sliding draw-bars are also visible on the doorways.

When in use, the hall would have had plastered walls, probably decorated with heraldic wall paintings, hanging tapestries and hunting trophies. The compacted earth floor would have been strewn with rushes, and scented with herbs to mask smells. Dogs were allowed to scavenge for scraps beneath the trestle tables set up within for banquets. The lord and his family would have sat on the raised dais and watched over the proceedings with light provided by flaming torches and candles.

Screens passage and buttery

At the far end of the hall, a wooden screen, placed just before the main doorway, concealed the working end. Behind the screen, the screens passage gave access to the kitchens via a covered corridor and to the small service room or buttery (from the French *bouteillerie* – bottle store) as well as to the stone stairs in the corner, which lead up to the parapet of the curtain wall outside. *Walk through into the buttery.*

Light was provided by two windows in the west gable wall. From this room the castle steward would have directed the servants (all male) and overseen the preparation of food and drink for the hall.

The solar

Above the buttery can be seen the wall of a first-floor apartment or solar (meaning a light and sunny room). This was a private space to which the lord and lady could retire from the bustle of the great hall. It is not clear how access was gained to it, but it is possible that there was an internal wooden staircase from the screens passage or buttery, or an external wooden staircase in the bailey. The solar was lit by three windows and had its own fireplace and latrine, both luxuries virtually unheard of in the district at the time the castle was rebuilt in the fourteenth century.

Return to the hall and take the exit in the far left of the 'screen' following ahead of you what was once the covered passageway, leading through a low arched doorway.

The south-western end of the great hall showing the opening on the left leading through to the kitchens; the remains of the stairs on the right that once led up to the parapet of the curtain wall outside, and the ruined wall visible beyond the screen

The hearth and ash pit in the first kitchen

One of the ovens, built into the base of the motte, at the furthest end of the kitchen

The interior of one of the large ovens

The passageway would once have been roofed to help keep the food warm as it was being carried from the kitchens to the hall.

The great hall and kitchen range were designed as separate buildings to allow a fire break between them, and to provide access from the bailey to the curtain wall beyond them.

Keep ahead to the kitchen range, which is the next block of buildings on your right.

THE KITCHENS

What you see now dates largely from the later period of the castle's occupation, as the kitchens underwent considerable alteration and extension over the centuries. The wall running at an angle was one of the last additions, but it is not known if this carried a roof or simply screened off the kitchen area from the bailey.

Enter the first kitchen on your right. The visible remains of a hearth and ash pit date from the late fourteenth or early fifteenth century but probably overlie earlier features. Above can be seen the remains of a high window. At the other end of the room a paved floor slopes away to a drain cut through the wall. Evidence of the food prepared in the kitchen was found during excavations, consisting of large quantities of bones from the best cuts of pig (especially skulls from boars' heads), sheep, cattle and deer. A wide variety of

freshwater and sea fish were also found, along with remains of hare, rabbit, poultry, game birds and various shellfish. The deer and game were no doubt from the Courtenay's own deer park, and it is known from documentary evidence that there were also large fishponds in the park. There were probably two cooking fires in here, one for spit-roasting meat and poultry and the other for cooking stews and broths. The ash pit was used for keeping food warm. The roof was high to allow the smoke to escape and to reduce the risk of fire.

Leave this room and enter the next kitchen on your right.

This room has a dividing wall and a stone-lined pit in one corner, probably used for storage. The two large ovens in the far wall were part of a later extension built into the base of the motte. They had tiled floors and domed roofs lined with clay to retain heat. The narrow entrances would have been plugged when baking bread or pies. Heat was provided by burning faggots – bundles of brushwood – which were raked out when the desired temperature was reached. Adjacent to the doorway into this room is what appears to be the remains of a stairway, implying that there was an upper floor over at least part of the kitchen, although it would have been necessary to leave room for smoke to circulate at a higher level. The narrow room between this kitchen and the steps to the keep was another late medieval addition, possibly the 'larderhouse' referred to in an inventory of 1422. Beneath this building lie the remains of a thirteenth-century building, which enclosed a 2m-deep water cistern cut into the rock. Above this, a fourteenth-century lead water pipe was discovered which would have collected water draining from the base of the motte and carried it in the direction of the eastern lodgings at the lower end of the bailey.

Walk to the base of the steps leading up the side of the mound.

THE MOTTE

The mound, or motte, was one of the earliest features of the castle, constructed in the late eleventh century. The natural raised spur of land was increased by about a third of its original height by cutting a ditch around the base to the west and to the east (where you are standing now) and heaping the excavated shale onto the top. Its summit stands some 25m (80 feet) from the bottom of the ditch on its western side. The ditch on this side was 4m (13 feet) deep and presumably was crossed by a wooden bridge until it was filled in during the thirteenth century.

The motte and the substantial stone tower that was constructed on its summit must have been an impressive sight and provided a powerful message from the Norman barons to the surrounding Saxon population.

The ruins of the keep high on the motte

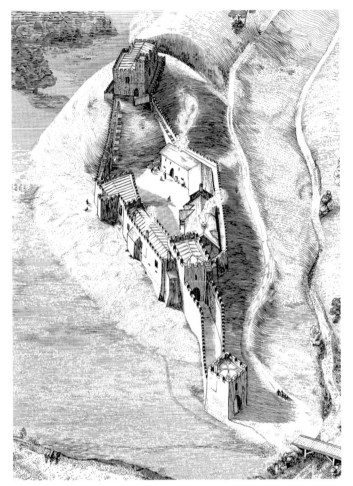

Reconstruction drawing of Okehampton Castle after it was rebuilt in the 14th century (S. Goddard)

The change of stonework in the front wall of the keep – a clue to its two-phase development

Middle Ages another path was built from the top via the remaining stone steps forming the lower part of the modern route, with some further steps leading up to a cobbled area outside the door to the keep.

THE KEEP

Ascend the stone steps and follow the path to the top.

From here there is a good view of the bailey layout below you. Turning round to examine the front wall of the keep, you will find a clue to its two-phase development. Notice the change of stonework half way up the left-hand part of the wall. It appears that a massive, square stone tower was built on this eastern end of the motte when it was constructed in the late eleventh century. Excavation has shown that solid stone foundations were set down at the same time that the upper layers of the motte were laid. The western half of the keep has no such foundations and was clearly a later addition, dated by its architectural features to the early

The steps that now ascend the side of the motte are comparatively modern. The route of the earliest access is unknown, but at the time of the fourteenth-century rebuilding, a set of steps climbed from the postern door in the south curtain wall to a path leading up to the summit. A scar on the face of the motte still reveals the route of this path. In the later

fourteenth-century rebuilding. Excavation failed to reveal whether any structure stood on the other half of the motte's summit when the Norman tower was constructed, although it is possible that there was some kind of timber structure there.

At the time of rebuilding, the earlier tower appears to have been partially dismantled to accommodate the stairs and turret to the right that gave access to the upper floor and the roof parapet. The thick walls were taken down to first-floor level and new walls built on top. There is no indication of a doorway into the Norman tower at ground level, and it was probably entered via wooden steps at right angles to a door at first-floor level. This arrangement would have made it very difficult for attackers to build up any momentum with a battering ram. The substantial nature of the walls and foundations, and other known examples of Norman towers, suggests that the original tower may have been three storeys in height. The entrance to the later keep was through the existing doorway. This may have had a short flight of steps leading up to the threshold, possibly enclosed by a small porch. A side door led to the stairs that were built into the thickness of the wall.

Step through the doorway into the first room.

Notice the early graffiti carved into the stones as you walk through. You can see the odd remnants of stone

steps still projecting from the curved inside wall of the gravity-defying ruined stairwell and turret. At ground-floor level you can see the remains of two widely splayed window openings similar to those in the ground-floor rooms throughout the castle, but there is little evidence of any features on the upper storey. The entrance to a garderobe can be seen built into the wall in the south-

The striking remains of the stair turret of the keep

THE GREAT DEER PARK

The Courtenays created a large deer park between the castle and the royal Forest of Dartmoor at about the time the castle was re-built in the early fourteenth century. The castle functioned more as a grand hunting lodge than as a defensive structure at this time, and a permanent staff would have looked after the 690 hectares (1,700 acres) of parkland as well as the deer and hounds.

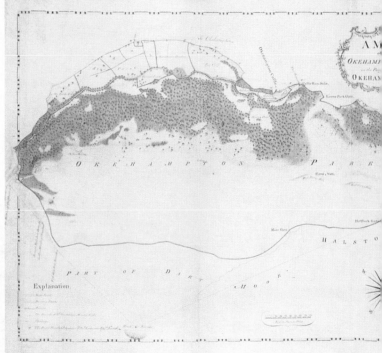

A fourteenth-century hunting scene

BRIDGEMAN ART LIBRARY/OSTERREISCHE NATIONAL BIBLIOTHEK, VIENNA.

The park was bounded by rivers and substantial banked walls and ditches, called deer leaps, which enabled deer to jump one way only. Trees were planted to provide cover. Ancient hollies and hawthorns can still be seen in parts of the old park. The deer were mainly roe deer. Larger red deer were the preserve of royalty. Other quarry would have included wild boar, foxes and hare. The hounds were probably kept in a field called Kennel Field near the castle. Horses would be stabled within the castle bailey. Earthwork remains at Saxon Gate on the hillside opposite the castle are those of a small building – possibly a small hunting lodge.

Preparations for the chase would have started well before dawn with grooms and kennel boys getting the horses and hounds ready and the keepers checking the park for poachers, any new hazards and the whereabouts of deer herds and

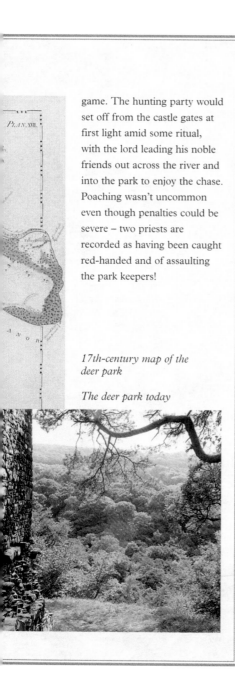

game. The hunting party would set off from the castle gates at first light amid some ritual, with the lord leading his noble friends out across the river and into the park to enjoy the chase. Poaching wasn't uncommon even though penalties could be severe – two priests are recorded as having been caught red-handed and of assaulting the park keepers!

17th-century map of the deer park

The deer park today

west corner, with its chute opening onto the motte outside. It is not clear whether the chute was continued over the side of the motte or whether someone had the unpleasant task of cleaning it out. The wall dividing this room from the inner one is very thick up to first-floor level. This represents another section of the original stone tower, with the thinner wall above dating from the rebuilding.

Walk through the opening into the inner room.

Notice the large joist holes for the floor and the projecting corbels higher up that probably supported a leaded roof. There are also patches of the original plaster still in place. In this room you get a clearer idea of the differences between the well-appointed upper rooms and the very basic accommodation afforded on the ground floor. The lower rooms were used either as stores or as servants' accommodation, although the lack of garderobes suggests the former. The windows were narrow to reduce the risk of entry by attackers, were unglazed and had deep interior splays to let in the maximum amount of light. By contrast, the upper floor windows were large, decorative and glazed, reflecting the high status of their occupants. In addition there is a fireplace and another garderobe built into the south-west corner. It can be assumed that these features were mirrored in the outer room. Unless there was a screened-off passage,

access to this upper room was presumably via the outer one. This suggests that this was the main room, either accommodation for the lord and lady or one of two lodgings for high-ranking guests. The views over the deer park would have been particularly fine from these rooms.

Although strongly built and in a good defensive position, the keep is not a true keep, like those of Dover Castle or the Tower of London, in that it was not self-contained enough to withstand a long siege. There would have been no water supply, kitchens or service rooms and, just as importantly, no chapel to sustain the spirit. The original motte and tower were certainly well placed: at this time, before the development of artillery, a straight assault up the steep slopes would have been foolhardy against a well-defended garrison.

The inner room of the keep showing windows and fireplaces on the ground and first floors. It would have commanded impressive views of the deer park

The 'true' keep of the Tower of London. The keep at Okehampton could not have withstood a long siege as this one could have done

BRIDGEMAN ART LIBRARY

If you wish, you can walk around the outside of the keep to appreciate the landscape and the defensive setting, but take care of the steep drops. Return to the bailey via the steps.

As you descend, notice the short stretch of curtain wall on your right, dating from the fourteenth century. It is very thick (1.8m or 6 feet) at the base and has a parapet on top with a thinner wall on its outside edge. This probably had crenellations (openings) in it to form a battlement. The wall may have extended up the motte side to the keep but, unlike the north curtain wall, it did not extend to encompass all the buildings on this side of the bailey. Instead, the high outer walls of the buildings themselves formed the defences with a steep bank below and marshy

ground beyond making attack from this side difficult. The area at the base of the motte on this side was initially left open and a communal garderobe was provided in the curtain wall. Close by the base of the motte and the earlier route to the keep is a small opening or postern gate. This could be used to make a discreet escape or to enable small raiding parties to leave the castle if it came under siege without compromising the overall security of the defences.

At the bottom of the steps turn right and enter the ruins of the western lodging.

Western lodging

The extensive lodgings on this side of the castle bailey served as guest accommodation when the noble owners were in residence. In keeping with this function they were quite luxurious for their time, with many windows for maximum light, and elaborate toilet arrangements.

Notice how well the walls were constructed and how the building was extensively altered during its history. The lodging was constructed in the late fourteenth or early fifteenth century on the space created by the infilling of the motte ditch. The base of the motte itself was cut back to make more space, with a revetment wall to stabilise it. Excavation revealed deep foundations and fragments of aplite and beerstone from the windows. The original

The postern gate in the southern wall of the castle

View of the western lodging, priest's lodging and chapel from the motte

The old millstone used in the building of the oven in the western lodging

Part of the 17th-century engraving of Okehampton Castle by the Buck brothers showing the old mill outside the barbican gate

lease, as extensive alterations were made to the lodging at this time. Flour for this may have been provided by a corn mill, which once stood in the meadow by the river. A recess was formed in the north wall and the original entrance was blocked by the large oven, with a broken millstone forming part of its base and another, smaller oven built in the thickness of the wall. A new entrance was formed in the wall on the north side. A porch, with stone footings that can still be seen, was added, and another entrance was created in the south wall by knocking through the garderobe. The alterations to this part of the castle were part of a huge scheme of alterations affecting all the buildings in the bailey including the priest's lodging and the kitchen range on the other side.

entrance to the ground floor was on the west side, where the base of an oven now stands. An external wooden staircase rose from the north-east, over the present entrance on the north side, and gave access to the upper floor. Both ground floor and upper floor had garderobes: the waste chutes from these can be seen side-by-side in the north wall.

The castle was abandoned in 1538 but, in 1682, parts of it were leased in connection with the working of a bakehouse. It is possible that this building was the bakehouse referred to in the

Leave the lodging via the opposite (south) entrance.

You can see the postern gate and garderobe in the curtain wall along the narrow passage to your right.

Turn left and enter the priest's lodging.

Priest's lodging

This small, narrow lodging probably provided accommodation for the family's chaplain. Strict religious observance was central to the castle's daily life, so it was important that the priest's accommodation was right next to the chapel. For the same reason, the lodging had two entrances, one from the western lodging (where you entered) and the other directly from the chapel. Little survives of the outer wall but there was a garderobe on the ground floor and it can be assumed that there was

a window and a fireplace at first-floor level. Notice the line of the sloping lead roof at the western end and the line of the later, seventeenth-century roof beneath it. The small outward projection at the eastern end may have been some kind of defensive feature as it provided a view along the southern walls of the buildings beyond. Alternatively it may have been a stair turret or even contained the castle's bells (see page 29).

Walk through into the chapel.

The east end of the priest's lodging with the remains of the crenellated wall top

The remains of the west wall of the priest's lodging showing the line of the original sloping roof and the later 17th-century roofline cut in below

Reconstruction drawing of the interior of the castle chapel in the early 14th century by Ivan Lapper

The remains of some medieval wall paintings can still be distinguished in the right conditions on the inside edge of the south-facing chapel window

The chapel interior from the south-west

Chapel

The eastern end still stands to its full height, though much of the western half has collapsed. The main entrance to the chapel was from the bailey to the north and had a porch, the eastern wall of which can still be seen. The wall tops of the chapel were crenellated, and a sloping lead roof would have been supported on corbels, some of which are still visible. A decorated wooden screen would have separated the chancel at the eastern end from the main body of the chapel. The altar was possibly supported on projecting corbels, the broken ends of which can be seen on the east wall. A third corbel above may have supported a statue. The two

surviving windows contain the remains of tracery in the decorated gothic style that was prevalent in churches of the

naval officer, Giles A. Vincent, was held on free parole in the town in 1809 following his capture at sea on 10th June that year. He was a surgeon on the French Man o' War, '*Rejoirie*'. Such officers were given relative freedom within a mile radius of their parole town as long as they attended a daily roll call. He was obviously attracted by the romantic ruins and left his mark – 'HIC V ... FUIT CAPTIVUS BELLI' (here Vincent was a prisoner-of-war).

Leave the chapel and turn right in the bailey, taking care on the cobbles and steeply sloping grass banks. Enter the first of the three eastern lodgings.

Eastern lodgings

Notice the first floor entrance from ground level outside the chapel. A complex garderobe arrangement in the far corner served both upper and lower rooms and those of the adjoining lodging in a block that projected out from the outer wall with a shared collection pit. The provision

district at this time. Some barely distinguishable wall paintings can also be found on the plaster on the inside edge of the south-facing window. These may have been heraldic or, perhaps, religious images. If you look closely at the wall plaster to the right of this window you may be able to pick out a grid-work of red lines that were painted onto the surface in imitation of ashlar blocks.

To the left of the window is the piscina (a shallow basin used to wash sacred vessels during the service of mass). This drained through the wall. An interesting piece of graffiti was carved into the face of the stone on the right-hand side during the Napoleonic Wars. A young French

Graffiti carved into the wall of the chapel during the Napoleonic wars

The south-facing chapel window with the piscina on the left of it

High in the wall, on what would have been the first floor, this stone washbasin can be seen built into the wall of the large garderobe chamber at the lower end of the eastern lodgings

The openings to the luxurious ground and first floor garderobes in the eastern lodgings

The interior of the eastern lodgings showing the openings for windows, garderobes and fireplaces

of garderobes for the ground floor rooms suggests that they were servants' quarters. Narrow, deeply splayed, unglazed windows at this level again provided light without compromising security, while the upper floor was lit by large arched windows in the north and south walls and heated by a fireplace in the south wall. Like the chapel, the wall tops were crenellated. The drip course of the shallow-pitched lead roof and some of the corbels that supported it are still visible. The second roof line

visible in the western wall probably dates from seventeenth-century re-occupation.

Leave this room by the same door and continue down the bailey to the adjoining lodgings.

The two upper rooms here were as well provided with windows and toilet arrangements as the first. The doors to the upper rooms were on the outside wall immediately above the ground-floor doors from the bailey, indicating that access was either from stairs on the outside of this wall, or via a gallery stretching all the way from the great hall opposite around the inner wall of the gatehouse. Each upper room had a window in its southern and western walls, as well as a window looking over the bailey. The garderobes can be seen in the far corner adjoining that of the lodgings on the higher side. The lower first-floor room appears to have had the most elaborate sanitary arrangements of the whole castle. Under a stone vaulted roof can be seen a small stone washbasin built into the wall and, to the right, the recessed garderobe with slots for a wooden seat. The front of the chute beneath has fallen away to reveal the shaft. The area beneath was probably a storeroom.

Return across the bailey and pass through the gap between the great hall and the kitchens.

CURTAIN WALL

Some idea of the scale of the early fourteenth-century defensive curtain wall can be gained from here. This would have been surmounted by a parapet, probably reached via the stairs in the north-west corner of the great hall. Three sockets in the outer face of the hall's north wall at its eastern end suggest that there may have been a timber walkway behind the curtain wall. The wall itself is 1.8m (6 feet) wide and originally extended from the base of the motte to the gatehouse, with a narrow gap between it and the buildings it

enclosed. The fourteenth-century wall overlies an earlier curtain wall, of a similar width, which was bedded on a low bank of clay. The defensive features on this side of the castle were augmented by the stream, which was then somewhat wider, and by the natural slope. When the castle fell into ruin, natural subsidence of the bank, and the weight of fallen roof slates against it, caused parts of the curtain wall to collapse outwards. During the seventeenth century re-occupation, an additional entrance was made through the wall at this point.

Bear left beyond the curtain wall and descend the grassy slope.

Note the ornamental ponds in the stream. These are fairly modern, probably dating from the early

The remains of the huge curtain wall on the north-west side of the castle

The waterfalls created in the stream to the north-west of the castle in the early twentieth century

A stone head discovered in the castle ditch, probably from one of the castle buildings of the 12th century

PLYMOUTH
MUSEUMS

twentieth century. However, it is likely that a larger fishpond existed here in the sixteenth century. You get a good idea of how the motte was constructed from this point and how much of it is natural. You can also appreciate the effort that must have gone into cutting the ditch into the rock beyond the motte and how daunting the castle would have appeared to a potential attacker from here.

Proceed along the path by the stream and follow it up to where it joins the field hedge and carry on up the slope for approximately 20m (66ft).
On the left are the remains of a small bank and ditch that may have been the western defences. These were either an outer defensive feature or the outer edge of an earlier or additional bailey.

Excavation failed to find any dating evidence or post holes that would have signified the existence of a timber palisade on the top of the bank. However, these may have been destroyed with the erosion of the bank into the ditch. It is also possible that the striking topography of the natural spur may have attracted attention before the arrival of the Normans and that these earthworks are part of an earlier enclosure. Fragments of tiles of a fabric similar to Roman ones found elsewhere in Devon were found in the fill of the motte ditch. These must have come from near the castle. A male stone head was also discovered in the ditch. It has been dated stylistically to the twelfth century and assumed to have been discarded from the Norman tower or another early castle building. However, it is also similar to carved heads that formed part of a pagan cult of the human head throughout northern Europe in the Iron Age. It bears classic Celtic features and it is tempting to consider a link with a pagan shrine in a sacred enclosure on the end of the spur.

The field to the right of the hedge is called Raynard's Field. The stream has its source in this field and an ancient trackway can be seen crossing it away from the castle. The field could be named after Rainer, Baldwin's steward, or the colloquial name for a fox (from the French *renard*).

WOODLAND WALK

From this point you can continue along the circular woodland walk which is about 1.6km (1 mile) and will take approximately 30 minutes, or you can retrace your steps along the path back to the ticket office. If you continue into the woods, the path is steep and uneven in places and there are steep drops to the side, so take extra care, especially with children. A trail, explaining the natural history of the woods, is available from the ticket office.

If you continue through the woods, you will return through the meadow on the south side of the motte from where you will get a good view of the castle's southern defences. Note the small window openings in the lower half of the high walls and the strong, battered wall bases standing on the steep banks. The backs of the fireplaces in the eastern lodgings can be seen projecting on supporting corbels on either side of the central garderobe block. It is possible to get a similar view to that shown in the eighteenth-century engraving by the brothers Samuel and Nathaniel Buck (see page 35) by crossing the river via the lane and footbridge just before the car park.

The north-eastern wall of the castle from the east

The exterior of the priest's lodging from the north-east

The Woodland Walk when the bluebells are out in May with the castle in the distance

HISTORY OF
THE CASTLE

NORMAN STRONGHOLD

With the prospect of open rebellion
across the South West, William the
Conqueror appointed one of his most
powerful and trusted barons, Baldwin
de Brionne, as Sheriff of Devon.
Baldwin – the son of a Norman count –
was married to William's cousin,
Emma. William granted him about
two hundred rural manors across
the county in return for his support,
and gave him the task of overseeing
the completion of the royal castle in
Exeter. He also allowed him to build
his own castle from which he could
oversee his new baronry.

*Normans building a castle
– scene from the Bayeux
Tapestry*

MICHAEL HOLFORD

Okehampton suited his purpose well
as it was at the centre of his estates,
and sat on one of the main routes
west into Cornwall, near the
confluence of several other important
routes. Dartmoor, to the south, was
still largely impenetrable. The site
chosen was on a natural spur that lent
itself to the creation of a classic
motte-and-bailey castle that would
dominate the nearby Saxon
settlement of Ocmundtune.

Baldwin's castle consisted of a
high, steep-sided motte, formed from
material thrown up from a deep
ditch that was cut from the rock
surrounding the highest point of the
spur. This was surmounted by a tall
stone tower, probably three storeys in
height and square in plan. A wooden
stockade probably surrounded it and
the bailey, and there may also have
been a wooden extension to the keep.
Any trace of this would have been
destroyed by the later stone
extension. A ditch and bank about
200m (218 yards) to the west may
have formed the outer defences of
another bailey on that side. Its other

sides were protected by the steep, natural slopes of the spur, or it may have simply provided an extra defensive feature. There would probably have been other buildings of stone or timber within the bailey, although no trace of these has been found in excavations.

Baldwin, no doubt, had more than a military stronghold in mind when he established the castle. By 1086, the Domesday survey records the existence of a market – one of only two recorded in Devon – and four burgesses (free townsmen). It also mentions a mill – also something of a rarity in Devon at that time – so, clearly, he was keen to encourage commerce and the development of a town with free traders who would provide taxes in return for certain privileges. The villeins (tenant farmers) living on the scattered farms throughout the parish, on the other hand, still had to fulfil their feudal obligation of working on Baldwin's home farm for an agreed number of days each year. Baldwin himself had to pay taxes and provide military

Okehampton Castle in the 14th century by Terry Ball

support to the king in return for his own grants of land which, like most baronies, were scattered across the county as a safeguard against insurrection from a consolidated power base. In this way William the Conqueror gained a firm grasp of his newly acquired realm in a fairly short space of time and with relatively few direct supporters.

Extract from the Domesday Book (1086-87), mentioning Okehampton

Both the market and burgesses are referred to in the Domesday entry for Okehampton, which suggests that a new town existed, although precisely where it was situated is unclear. It could have been at the castle gates, thereby enjoying its protection and patronage to the disadvantage of the Saxon settlement of Ocmundtune or it may have become established between the two rivers in its present location – midway between castle and church and straddling the main highway. Wherever its exact location, the infant town of Okehampton grew under the patronage of the Sheriff and his heirs. When Baldwin died in 1090 he left four sons. Guiger was a monk at Bec Abbey in Normandy while William, Robert and Richard were all actively involved with his estates and were also sheriffs. Robert concentrated on affairs back in Normandy, while William and Richard went on to assist with the conquest of South Wales. Okehampton Castle was never the permanent residence of any of them but Richard is said to have been the founder of the 'ancient customs' referred to in a charter granted to the borough by Robert Courtenay after he came into the estate in 1219.

THE COURTENAYS

None of Baldwin's sons had any male heirs and so their sister, Adeliza, succeeded them. The castle and other estates then passed through the families of various heiresses until 1173 when the surviving heiress, Hawisia, married Reginald Courtenay – so beginning the long association between the Courtenay family and the castle. The various owners during the intervening period appear to have taken little interest in Okehampton or the castle. Unlike other Devonian castles, Okehampton does not feature in records of the civil war during Stephen's reign (1135-54). With the acquisition of the barony of Okehampton, the Courtenays'

Map of the hamlets of Okehampton Parish

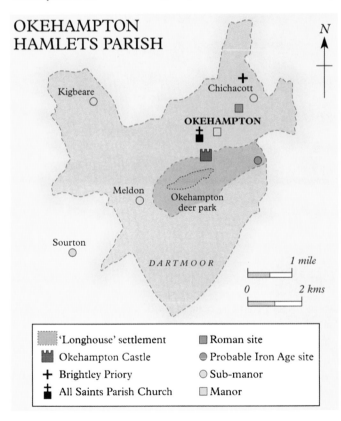

OKEHAMPTON HAMLETS PARISH

N

Kigbeare

Chichacott

OKEHAMPTON

Meldon

Okehampton deer park

Sourton

DARTMOOR

1 mile

0   2 kms

'Longhouse' settlement	■ Roman site
Okehampton Castle	● Probable Iron Age site
✚ Brightley Priory	○ Sub-manor
All Saints Parish Church	▢ Manor

fortunes were secured. Reginald Courtenay's son, Robert, inherited the estates in 1190 and his marriage to Mary, daughter of William de Vernon, the fifth Earl of Devon, was eventually to bring the title Earl of Devon and further estates to the family. Robert was Sheriff of Devon for some time. In 1193-94, the castle was briefly in royal hands, along with Launceston Castle, while King Richard was actively strengthening castle defences in the face of threats from his brother John and from France. In about 1219, Robert granted a charter to the borough of Okehampton, confirming the old rights of the burgesses (freemen) 'which they had in the time of Richard the son of Baldwin'. He also granted various other privileges including the right to elect a provost (*portreeve*) and an assistant known as the cryer. The provost would collect market tolls for the lord as well as representing the interests of the burgesses. The burgesses were able to avoid the usual feudal obligations of military or other service in return for suitable payment and the Courtenays thus encouraged the growth of the young borough.

Robert died in 1242 and was succeeded by John Courtenay. Various modest structures were built in the castle bailey during the twelfth and early thirteenth centuries. Excavations in the surviving fourteenth-century great hall revealed the foundations of a square building beneath the service end, which probably dated from the late twelfth century. The clay-bonded walls of a building of a slightly later date were found beneath the main body of the hall. In about the middle of the thirteenth century, the ditch between the motte and the bailey appears to have been filled in and stone structures placed within it. A water cistern was also cut into the base of the motte. Stretches of an earlier curtain wall are preserved to the north of the kitchens and hall.

Although no archaeological investigation has taken place on the southern side of the bailey, the absence of structures in the centre of the bailey suggests that the earlier buildings were ranged around an open space in a similar fashion to those of the fourteenth-century rebuilding.

In 1274, after John Courtenay's death, the castle was described as 'an old motte which is worth nothing, and outside the motte a hall, chamber and kitchen...'. This is not necessarily a completely faithful description of the buildings that existed then, but it is the best surviving documentary reference from the period.

Nearby Launceston Castle, a contemporary of Okehampton

Shield of Robert de Courtenay, Baron of Okehampton (died 1242)

BRIDGEMAN ART LIBRARY/BRITISH LIBRARY COTT. CLAUD D II F. 113

King John hunting from a painting of about 1321. Deer hunting was a favourite pastime of royalty and noblemen at this time

Shield of Hugh Courtenay (died 1291) who is thought to have planned the redevelopment of the deer park

The ruins of Tiverton Castle, once the principal home of the Courtenays when the role of Okehampton shifted from defensive stronghold to hunting retreat

Hugh Courtenay and the Deer Park

The Courtenay family's principal home had become Tiverton Castle, the former seat of the de Vernon family, from whom they had obtained the earldom of Devon. The role of Okehampton Castle had shifted from that of secure military stronghold in case of local rebellion, towards a country retreat, where the family could enjoy hunting and other activities and impress guests with their wealth. It was important, therefore, that the deer park and accommodation were fitting for an earl. John's son, Hugh Courtenay, appears to have planned the extension and redevelopment of the castle's deer park. He prepared an agreement with the burgesses whereby they relinquished their grazing rights in his wood to the south of the castle in exchange for rights on the wastes which lay between it and the Forest of Dartmoor. On the hillside opposite the castle lay a scattered settlement of single-storeyed 'long houses' (a cross passage dividing the 'shippon' or cow house from the living area). This probably represented the arable lands referred to as 'Byrham' in the document. The relatively mild climate of the twelfth and thirteenth centuries had enabled cultivation on such high exposed ground and the settlement had grown steadily over the previous hundred years or so. The creation of the extended deer park, combined

TIVERTON CASTLE

Aerial view of part of the medieval long house settlement still visible in the deer park near Okehampton Castle

lived to an advanced age, dying in London on 30 September 1328. Presumably she enjoyed the hunt as much as her late husband did, for two bells were cast bearing the old English inscriptions: 'We were both made to wake Eleanor for to catch game' and 'But do by my advice think on Hugh's soul and so was his name'. It is assumed these referred to Eleanor and Hugh Courtenay, and they may well have been incorporated into the rebuilding of the castle in the early fourteenth century.

However, they later somehow found their way to the small parish church of Tresmeer, 13km (8 miles) to the west of Launceston in Cornwall. After the Reformation of the mid-sixteenth century (not long after the castle was abandoned), the living of Okehampton parish was transferred to the Russell family, who were also patrons of Tresmeer parish. Perhaps Tresmeer was in need of bells and the redundant pair from the castle was thus commandeered for the purpose. The bells have been dated to the early fourteenth century, which supports

with deterioration in the climate, probably led to its abandonment at the end of the thirteenth century. It is possible that the tenants were forcibly evicted.

The Courtenay bells

Hugh certainly appears not to have been a man to cross. On one occasion he fell out with the monks of Forde Abbey – the house founded by his ancestors – and raided their cattle, driving them out onto the wastes of Dartmoor. Hugh died in 1291, although his widow, Lady Eleanor,

One of the two 14th-century 'Courtenay' bells now in the care of the Museum of Dartmoor Life. These were thought to have been associated with Okehampton and the inscriptions engraved around them apparently refer to Hugh Courtenay and his wife Eleanor

the theory that they may have been made for the castle, as it is very unusual to find secular inscriptions on bells of this period. At the time of writing, Tresmeer Parish has loaned the bells to the Museum of Dartmoor Life in Okehampton for conservation work and eventual display in the museum.

Hugh II and the rebuilding of the castle

Hugh and Eleanor's son Hugh II was still a minor on his father's death and a ward of King Edward and so the castle was in royal hands until he came of age in 1297. During this time, the castle was maintained and there are records of lead, tiles, nails and lime being bought for repairs as well as some work being done on the walls, but the Earldom was allowed to lapse. Hugh was finally granted the title of Earl of Devon by King Edward III in 1335, just five years before Hugh's death. In spite of this, as soon as Hugh inherited the castle, he set about rebuilding it to befit his status. Though Tiverton Castle was now the family's principal residence, it was common for the wealthiest families to have another residence used largely for entertaining. Okehampton's setting was ideal for this particularly because of the deer park. Hugh therefore set about creating an imposing castle where he could entertain his noble friends as well as carrying out the administration of the family's vast

Shield of Hugh II, Earl of Devon (died 1340), son of Hugh and Eleanor – one of many that encircle the dining room at Powderham Castle today. Hugh II is thought to have been responsible for the rebuilding of the castle in the early 14th century

estates through the offices of his steward. Although records are few, it is to this period that most of the standing remains of the castle can be attributed, with the exception of the western lodgings and the western extension to the kitchens. The great hall, with its central open hearth, was the focus for entertainment and feasting as well as housing the manor courts. Luxurious new lodgings were built to accommodate the family and guests. Unlike the servants' quarters, these were well appointed, with views over the deer park, elaborate latrines and enclosed fireplaces.

The advent of the chimney, and thus separate fireplaces, in the Middle Ages was to play a large part in the physical division of different social classes who had, for millennia, been forced to gather together around the communal fire.

Hugh II was an ambitious young man who became very active in national politics, including fierce opposition to King Edward II. Both Hugh and his wife Agnes died in 1340, and were buried together amid great ceremony in Cowick Priory. Their eldest son, John, became Abbot of Tavistock Abbey in 1334. His younger brother, also called Hugh, succeeded to the earldom and the Courtenay estates on his father's death, and married Margaret de Bohun, granddaughter of King Edward I. Powderham Castle passed to the Courtenay family as dowry and has been the principal residence of the family from then until the present day. Hugh III became one of the original Knights of the Garter and was buried in Exeter Cathedral in 1377. He and Margaret had no fewer than nine daughters and eight sons and William, their fourth son, achieved the highest rank in the medieval English Catholic Church as the Archbishop of Canterbury.

Hugh III was succeeded as Earl by his grandson Edward, the 'Blind Earl' (*c.*1357–1419) and Hugh IV who died in 1422.

As one of the most powerful families in the South West, and as they were very prominent in national affairs, the Courtenays' stays at Okehampton would have been infrequent. However, life at the castle would have carried on under the direction of the constable and lord's steward. A permanent staff would have looked after the buildings and family affairs such as manor courts, rent collection and legal matters pertaining to the tenants. When the family were in residence, the numbers would swell considerably. Occasionally the lords' 'familiars' would attend the castle en masse. These were people bound to the family by marriage or patronage and, along with household and administrative servants, numbered over one hundred. In the 1380s, the

POWDERHAM CASTLE

familiars of Edward Courtenay (the 'Blind Earl') included eight knights, 41 esquires (trainee knights), 14 lawyers, eight beneficed clergymen, three damsels (young ladies of rank) and 61 servants. The latter would have looked after Okehampton and Tiverton castles and served Edward's itinerant household. The number of familiars would have grown as the family's power and influence grew and, no doubt, this explains the need for the extensions to the castle's accommodation that were constructed during the late fourteenth and fifteenth centuries. Upkeep also continued and, as records show,

Powderham Castle, Devon, became the main home of the Courtenay family when Hugh III married Margaret de Bohun, granddaughter of King Edward I, in the mid-14th century. It is still the principal residence of the Courtenay family today

The seal of Hugh Courtenay, 4th Earl of Devon, 1421

Shield of Edward Courtenay III (died c.1370), the father of the 'Blind Earl'

Shield of Thomas Courtenay, 5th Earl of Devon (died 1458)

Shield of Thomas Courtenay, 6th Earl of Devon, who fought for King Henry VI at Northampton and Wakefield in 1460 but was beheaded soon after

Edward Courtenay medal

BRITISH MUSEUM

window glass was bought in 1379-80 and various buildings in the castle were re-roofed in slate, quarried on a Courtenay manor in nearby Bridestowe in 1422.

The rise and fall of the Courtenays

The lives of the Courtenays, as one of the most powerful and influential families in the land, were far removed from the unrelenting hardships of life for the majority of people. However, during their infrequent stays at the Castle, the Courtenays were to spend much of their time in preparation for the latest hostilities in the Wars of the Roses.

Thomas Courtenay, the fifth Earl of Devon, and a ward of King Henry VI, married Margaret, the daughter of the first Earl of Somerset, quarrelled with the Earl of Arundel, fought with Lord Bonville and pillaged Exeter Cathedral. He initially fought for the Yorkist cause but, having been impeached for treason in 1454, obtained a pardon and eventually died in 1458 while in attendance on the King. His son, Thomas, the sixth earl, fought for King Henry VI at Northampton and Wakefield in 1460 but was captured at Towton the following year and beheaded. Okehampton and the

other estates were briefly forfeited to King Edward IV until Henry's return to the throne when they were restored to Thomas's son, John. John was subsequently killed at the battle of Tewkesbury in 1471, and various other members of the family were to be either killed in battle or beheaded. The earldom was eventually restored to Edward Courtenay, grandson of Sir Hugh Courtenay of Haccombe and Boconoc.

For a while the Courtenays seemed to be in favour with the Crown again. Indeed William, the eighth earl, even married Katherine, daughter of King Edward IV, but was later imprisoned in the Tower of London, together with his son and grandson. He was released by King Henry VIII on his accession to the throne and the earldom was restored once again. Sadly, William died just before the investiture, but the king allowed him to be buried as an earl. His son, Henry, the ninth earl, attained the greatest status of any in the family before him when King Henry VIII created him Marquis of Exeter. At first the two men were great friends – perhaps too close, for the King's sense of insecurity led him to accuse the Marquis of entering a conspiracy with Cardinal Pole. The ninth earl was attainted and beheaded on 9th January 1539. With his death ended the family's long association with Okehampton Castle as a great residence. The estates were once again

POWDERHAM CASTLE

NATIONAL PORTRAIT GALLERY

King Henry VIII showed great favour to Henry Courtenay, but eventually had him beheaded

Henry Courtenay, 9th Earl of Devon (died 1539), was created Marquis of Exeter by Henry VIII, but was eventually beheaded by him. This portrait hangs in the dining room at Powderham Castle

suggest abandonment, decay and collapse, perhaps hastened by local builders who would have made good use of any materials they could salvage. Small hearths for melting lead from the roofs and windows have been discovered in the great hall and the removal of the beerstone columns that supported the gatehouse must have caused it to collapse. On Edward Courtenay's death in 1556, the estates were divided among the descendants of the four sisters of Edward, the seventh earl, who had died in 1509. These families were the Arundells, Trethurffes, Mohuns, Vivians, Bullers and Trelawnys. Meanwhile, the burgesses of Okehampton, in the absence of a powerful resident landowner, were anxious to assert their independence, and commenced the long and expensive business of purchasing the rights to the borough and market from these families.

From 1623, when the town was granted a charter by James I, until the borough was disenfranchised in 1831, ownership of the castle also carried parliamentary privileges. Among the more notable holders of Okehampton's two precious parliamentary seats were Lord Clive of India, William Pitt the Elder (British Prime Minister and later the Earl of Chatham) and members of the Spencer family (ancestors of Lady Diana Spencer). However, none of these families seems to have taken much interest in the castle

confiscated and the great hunting park abandoned. Despite no charge being levelled against him, the Marquis's son, Edward, was sent to the Tower where he remained until the accession of Queen Mary. The earldom was restored yet again and it was even suggested that he might marry the Queen but, as had been the case for so many of his ancestors, fortune turned against him and he was exiled to Padua where he died in 1556.

THE CASTLE IN DECAY

There is no evidence to suggest that the castle was deliberately dismantled. Accumulations of slate and rubble

Shield of Edward Courtenay, Earl of Devon (died 1556), imprisoned in the Tower because his father had fallen out of favour with Henry VIII

❖ THE GHOST OF LADY HOWARD ❖

The castle has long been associated with the legend of Lady Howard, a seventeenth-century heiress to the Courtenay estates and daughter of Sir John Fitz of Fitzford House, Tavistock. She is said to have murdered three of her four husbands and two of her children, although there appears to be no historical basis for this. In one version of the legend, her penance is to travel nightly from her father's house to the castle grounds in a coach made of her victims' bones, preceded by a spectral hound with a single burning eye and there to pick a single blade of grass and take it home. Only when she has succeeded in removing every blade, or the world comes to an end, will her task be complete and her soul rest in peace. An old ballad runs: -

My Ladye hath a sable coach
With horses two and four.
My Ladye hath a gaunt blood-hound
That goeth on before.
My Ladye's coach hath nodding
plumes
The driver hath no head.
My Ladye is an ashen white
As one who is long dead.

itself. Unlike other abandoned medieval castles in Devon, the castle ruins do not appear to have featured at all in the Civil War of the mid-seventeenth century. Forces from both sides did, however, make encampments in and around the town at different times and there was a small battle fought on Sourton Down in May 1643.

Parts of the castle were re-occupied in the late seventeenth century when a man named John Ellacott (later Mayor of Okehampton) appears to have set up a bakehouse in the old western lodgings under a lease dated 1682. This may have been run in conjunction with a double water mill near the old barbican gate, which

THE SOUTH VIEW OF OKEHAMPTON–CASTLE, IN THE COUNTY OF DEVON.

This Castle, was built by Baldwin de Brionys, & was at first call'd Ochementon; it descended to Rich. de Rivers or Riparius, & from him to his Sister Adeliza, who marrying one of the Courtenays, it came into that Noble Family, & so continued till K.E. IV. seized it for their adherance to the House of Lancaster K.H. VII. restord it to the Courtenays, but K.H.VIII. again alienated it & dismantled the Castle & Park, yet Ed. Courtenay in Q. Marys Raign obtain'd a Restoration, but he dying without Issue Male, it came by a Female into the Mohuns Barons of Mohun & Okehampton, & by the like failure of male it came by marriage to Christopher Barrns of Doynes Esq.r
S. & N. Buck, delin. et sculp.

features in an eighteenth-century engraving by Samuel and Nathaniel Buck. The lease refers to 'that gatehouse first entering the old decayed castle of Okehampton' and other rooms. Evidence was found of re-use of the castle in the chapel and priest's lodging, as well as the western lodgings and one of the east lodgings. A garden had been laid out in part of the kitchen range.

THE LAST THREE HUNDRED YEARS

The old deer park became woodland and pasture, with new enclosures laid out inside it during the eighteenth century. By this time the castle ruins were attracting the attentions of romantic painters such as J.M.W. Turner, as well as antiquarians and writers. A local benefactor, Mr. Sydney Simmons, acquired the castle in the early twentieth century and carried out some restoration work before passing it to the Okehampton Castle Trust in 1917. It was later placed in the care of the Ministry of Public Buildings and Works in 1967 and a programme of major consolidation works was carried out over the next thirty years. Archaeological investigations conducted by Dr. R.A. Higham of the University of Exeter in the 1970s added greatly to the knowledge of the site and its development. It has been in the care of English Heritage since 1984.

Engraving of Okehampton Castle by Samuel and Nathaniel Buck, 1734

Painting of Okehampton Castle by J.M.W. Turner, c.1824

TATE GALLERY

FURTHER READING

Austin D., *Excavations in Okehampton Deer Park, Devon 1976–1978.* Proceedings of the Devon Archaeological Society, 36 (1978).

Austin, D., Daggett, R.H. and Walker, M.J.C, *Farms and Fields in Okehampton Park, Devon: the Problems of Studying Medieval Landscape. Landscape History,* 2 (1980).

Endacott, A., *Tales of Old Ockington – Reliving 2000 years in Okehampton, a Dartmoor Town.* Orchard Publications, Chudleigh (2002).

Higham, R.A., *Okehampton Castle, Devon.* English Heritage, London (1984).

Higham. R.A., *Excavations at Okehampton Castle, Devon. Part 1: The Motte and Keep.* Reprinted from the Proceedings of the Devon Archaeological Society, 35 (1977).

Higham, R.A. and Allan, J.P., *Excavations at Okehampton Castle, Devon. Part 2: The Bailey. A Preliminary Report.* Proceedings of the Devon Archaeological Society, 38 (1980).

Higham, R.A. Allan, J.P. and Blaylock, S.R., *Excavations at Okehampton Castle, Devon, Part 2: The Bailey,* Proceedings of the Devon Archaeological Society, 40 (1982).

Planel. P., *Okehampton Castle. A Handbook for Teachers.* English Heritage, London (1992).

Worth, R.N., *Okehampton Castle,* Transactions of the Devonshire Association, 27 (1895).

Wright, W.H.K., *Some Account of the Baronry and Town of Okehampton: Its Antiquities and Institutions.* William Masland, Tiverton (1889).

Young, Edward H., *Parochial Histories of Devonshire: No. 1. Okehampton.* The Devonshire Association for the Advancement of Science, Literature and Art, Exeter (1931).